How to play

CROQ

a step·by·step guide

Series editor:
Mike Shaw

Technical consultant:
Nigel Aspinall
8 times Singles Champion,
British Open Championships

JARROLD

Other titles in this series are:

How to play TENNIS
BADMINTON
SQUASH
BOWLS
TABLE TENNIS

How to play CROQUET
ISBN 0-7117-0423-6
First published in Great Britain, 1989
Copyright © Mike Shaw, 1989

Designed and produced by
Parke Sutton Limited, 8 Thorpe Road,
Norwich NR1 1RY
for Jarrold Colour Publications, Barrack Street,
Norwich NR3 1TR
Illustrations by Malcolm Ryan

Printed in Portugal

Contents

Introduction

Croquet is a game suited to any age and can be played by boys and girls, men and women of all skill levels. As such, it is an ideal family game although it is also becoming increasingly popular at both club and competition level.

Despite its 'maiden aunt' image, croquet is a surprisingly skilful and complex game. It combines elements of snooker with the tactics of chess. This book will demonstrate how sophisticated even the basic moves can be and shows that mastery of the game of croquet is as much in the head as in the hands.

The equipment required is minimal and inexpensive and any reasonably sized, flat, well-cut lawn can be transformed into a croquet court for a game. If you wish to take the game seriously, there are a number of clubs throughout the country. More information can be obtained from your local County Council or the National Croquet Association.

Along with cricket and tennis, croquet perhaps epitomises a tranquil summer's afternoon sport. Once the relatively simple strokes have been mastered, the game is both fascinating and fun to play, even for relative newcomers to the game. But beware: it can also be highly competitive, particularly at more advanced levels, requiring concentration and skill over long periods. You may well find it more strenuous – and more challenging – than you anticipate, for both the brain and the body!

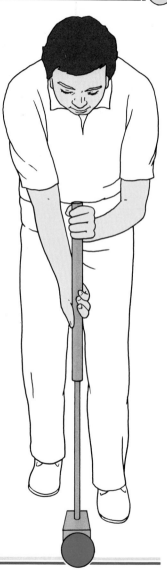

The Court

Croquet is played on grass which should be as flat and well maintained as possible. It is as well to try a few balls on a new court to see how the land lies. If one side tends to play out you will have to adjust your strokes accordingly, especially when playing close to the boundaries.

The full-sized croquet court is quite large and takes some getting used to. The small illustration shows the reduced dimensions generally used for domestic games.

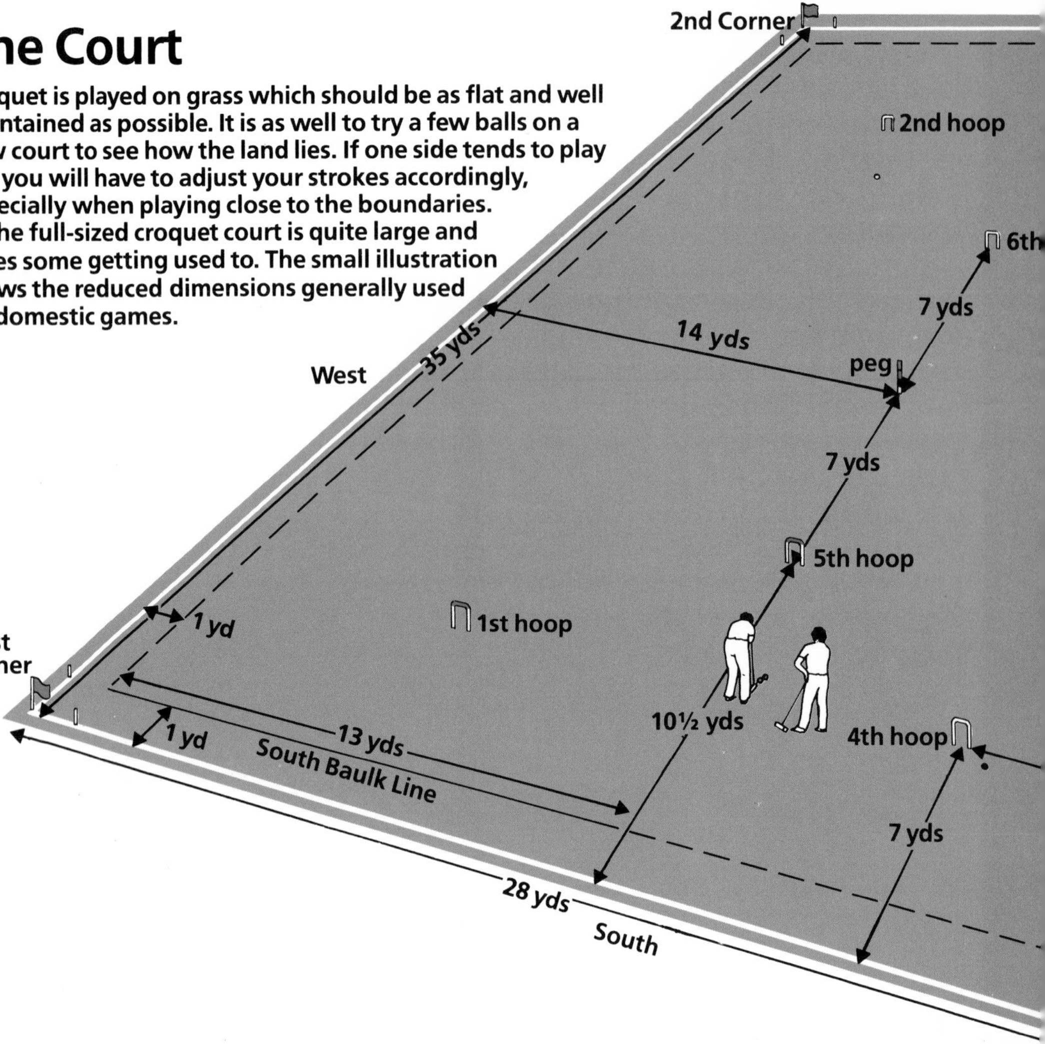

2nd Corner

2nd hoop

6th

7 yds

West

35 yds

14 yds

peg

7 yds

7 yds

5th hoop

1st hoop

1 yd

1st Corner

1 yd

13 yds

10½ yds

4th hoop

South Baulk Line

7 yds

28 yds

South

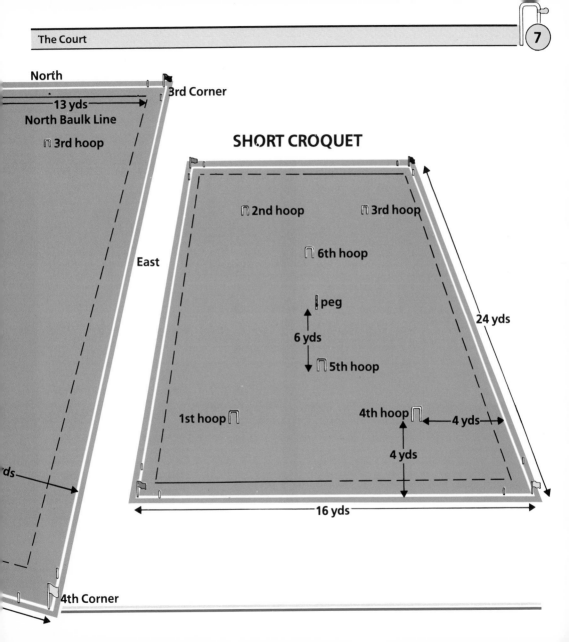

North

3rd Corner

13 yds

North Baulk Line

3rd hoop

SHORT CROQUET

2nd hoop   3rd hoop

6th hoop

East

peg

6 yds

5th hoop

24 yds

1st hoop

4th hoop   4 yds

4 yds

16 yds

yds

4th Corner

Equipment

Hoops

There are six hoops, usually
made of iron and painted
white.

Two of the hoops have
coloured tops – the first,
which is painted blue, and the
'Rover', which is painted red.

When buying a croquet set
make sure the hoops are solid
– often described as
'championship'. Feeble wire
varieties are useless.

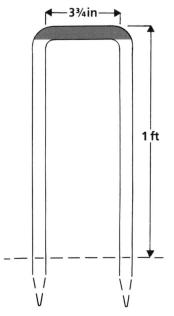

3¾ in

1 ft

Corner pegs

Eight wooden pegs are used to
mark the yard lines.

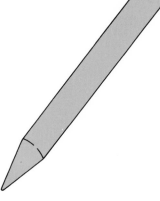

1 ft 6 in

The peg

The winning peg is made of
wood and painted white at the
bottom. It has four rings in the
colours of the four balls – blue,
red, black and yellow.

Hoop markers

Four spring clips, one in each of
the colours of the four balls,
are used to show which hoop a
ball has to go through next.
Every time a player 'scores' a
hoop with a ball the clip which
corresponds to the ball's colour
must be moved to the next
hoop to be run. Once all the
hoops have been 'scored' the
clip is moved to the winning
peg.

Balls

Four balls made of composite are used in the game, each weighing one pound. There is one blue, one black, one red and one yellow.

TEAM 1		TEAM 2	
blue	black	red	yellow

The width of the ball and the size of the hoop make for a tight squeeze, as there is only one-sixteenth of an inch clearance on each side.

◄——— 3⅝ in ———►

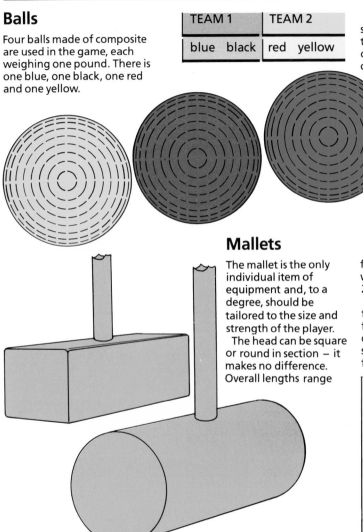

Mallets

The mallet is the only individual item of equipment and, to a degree, should be tailored to the size and strength of the player.

The head can be square or round in section – it makes no difference. Overall lengths range from 9 to 12 inches, and the weight of the head from 2lb-10oz to 3lb-10oz.

The length of the shaft varies from about 2½ feet to over 3 feet depending on the height of the player and the choice of style. Mallets may also vary in flexibility.

Dress

At all but the highest level dress is not an important consideration. Clubs, however, generally insist on completely flat-soled footwear to protect the court.

In tournaments, white is worn and competitors will need waterproofs as play does not stop except for heavy rain.

Scoring

The object is for one side to get both the balls through all the hoops before the other side in the sequence shown.

Starting

Players may start from either baulk line. The aim is to get both balls to pass through all the hoops in the sequence shown. One ball in a team does not have to wait for the other.

Playing out

One point is scored for running a ball through each hoop in sequence on the way out.

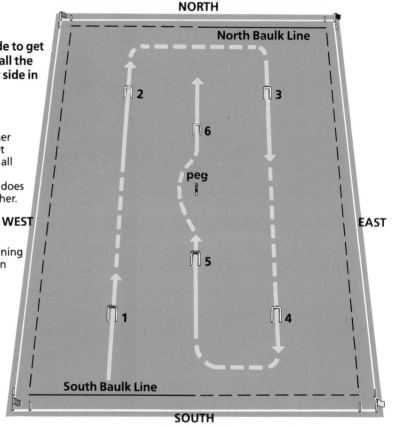

26 point games

Each side has two balls, consequently there are 12 points to be scored going out, 12 coming back, and 2 for hitting the peg – a total of 26.

14 point games

Usually played in short croquet, or for a half game. Play six hoops out and then the winning peg.

Playing back

On the way back one point is scored for running a ball through each correct hoop and one for hitting the winning peg.

Singles and doubles

The game can be played as singles or doubles. In the singles game one person plays both the balls in a side. In doubles the players take one ball each and only play their own ball.

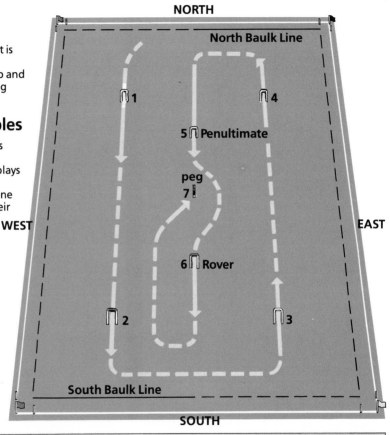

18 point games

1 Play the fifth and sixth hoops out, all six hoops and the peg back.

2 For a more complicated version, only possible in singles, one ball plays six out, six back, and the peg (13 points). The other ball starts at three back and plays to the peg (5 points).

The toss

A coin is tossed to see who starts and who plays with which balls. One side has the yellow and red balls, the other side, the blue and black pair.

The winner of the toss may choose either to start (or not), or which balls to play with. The loser makes the choice that is left. It is generally thought advantageous to start first, whereas the colour of the balls to be played with gives no advantage.

A turn

One side plays at a time, this is called 'a turn'. Either of a team's balls may be played during a turn, but once the choice is made only that ball may be struck. In doubles, therefore, the player to play depends on the ball chosen for the turn.

A turn consists of a single stroke, but extra strokes are earned if the ball played either strikes another ball — a roquet – or scores a hoop.

If the player fails to roquet or score a hoop then it is a miss, and the turn goes to the other side.

The Basic Shots

There are only three possible shots in croquet. A player must either roquet or score a hoop with the first shot of a turn or the turn is over.

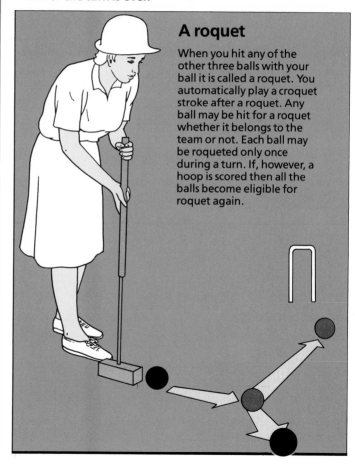

A roquet

When you hit any of the other three balls with your ball it is called a roquet. You automatically play a croquet stroke after a roquet. Any ball may be hit for a roquet whether it belongs to the team or not. Each ball may be roqueted only once during a turn. If, however, a hoop is scored then all the balls become eligible for roquet again.

Croquet

After a roquet the player's ball is picked up and placed so that it is touching the ball that has been roqueted.

The player's ball is then hit with the mallet. By this means both balls can be manoeuvred, as in snooker, to the desired position (see pages 24 and 25). Playing a croquet stroke automatically earns a free stroke (the continuation shot).

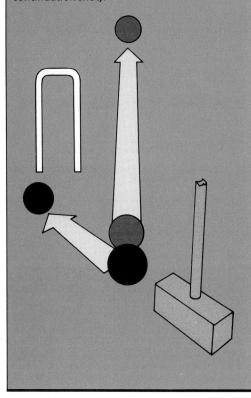

Scoring a hoop

The player strikes the ball so that it passes through the correct hoop in the sequence. This earns a point, another free stroke, and the freedom to roquet all the other balls again.

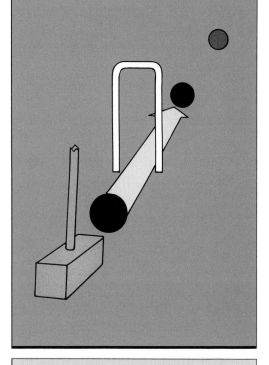

The various rules governing a miss, a roquet, a croquet and scoring a hoop are shown in the following pages.

A Miss

A miss is when your stroke fails either 1) to hit another ball (roquet)
or 2) to score (or run) a hoop.

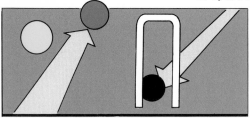

Consequences

● **End of turn**

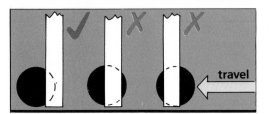

Get your opponent to use a mallet to judge if a ball has run a hoop.

If your ball goes over the yard-line

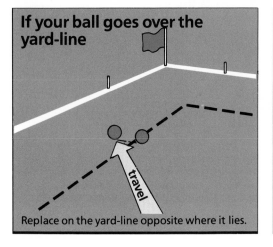

Replace on the yard-line opposite where it lies.

If your ball goes out of court

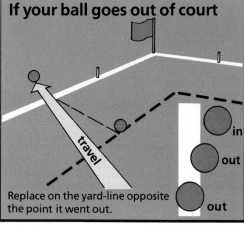

Replace on the yard-line opposite the point it went out.

A Roquet

A roquet is when your ball hits any of the other balls.

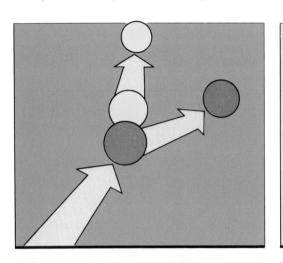

Consequences

- **You must take croquet off the ball you hit.**

If your ball crosses the yard-line

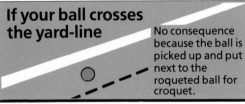

No consequence because the ball is picked up and put next to the roqueted ball for croquet.

If your ball goes out

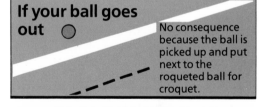

No consequence because the ball is picked up and put next to the roqueted ball for croquet.

If the roqueted ball crosses the yard-line

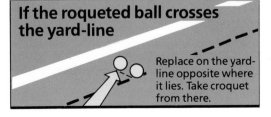

Replace on the yard-line opposite where it lies. Take croquet from there.

If the roqueted ball goes out

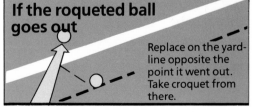

Replace on the yard-line opposite the point it went out. Take croquet from there.

A Croquet

A croquet stroke must be played after a roquet. Pick up your ball and place it so that it is touching the roqueted ball. NOTE: when playing this stroke the roqueted ball must be seen to move, even if it only shakes.

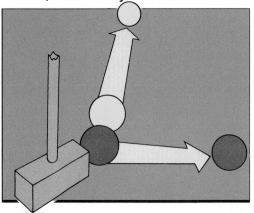

Consequences
- **You get another shot (the continuation shot).**
- **You may not roquet the ball again in this turn unless you run a hoop when all other balls become eligible again.**

If your ball crosses the yard-line

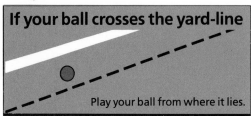

Play your ball from where it lies.

If your ball goes out

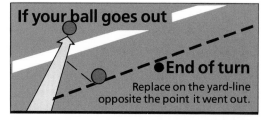

● **End of turn**

Replace on the yard-line opposite the point it went out.

If the croqueted ball crosses the yard-line

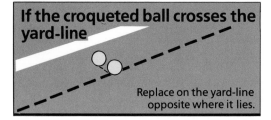

Replace on the yard-line opposite where it lies.

If the croqueted ball goes out

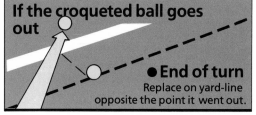

● **End of turn**

Replace on yard-line opposite the point it went out.

Running a Hoop

To run a hoop successfully the whole of the ball must have passed the front of the hoop so that when a flat surface is placed across the hoop the ball is clear.

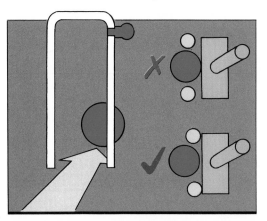

Consequences
- You score a point.
- Take your clip off the hoop.
- All balls become eligible for roquet again.
- You get another shot (a continuation shot).
- If you also hit another ball take croquet immediately.

If your ball goes over the yard-line

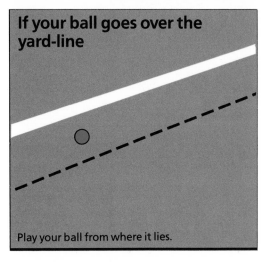

Play your ball from where it lies.

If your ball goes out

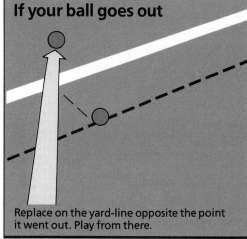

Replace on the yard-line opposite the point it went out. Play from there.

Faults

You can also lose your turn for any of the following reasons:-

1 Double hits

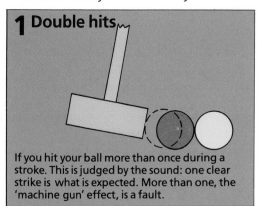

If you hit your ball more than once during a stroke. This is judged by the sound: one clear strike is what is expected. More than one, the 'machine gun' effect, is a fault.

2 Wrong ball

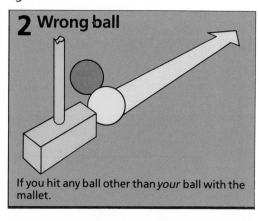

If you hit any ball other than *your* ball with the mallet.

3 Crush shot

If you play *a crush shot*. This is where one side of a hoop or the peg is in the way of the shot you wish to make. The crush occurs when the ball, the mallet and the obstruction are simultaneously in contact. You must play away from an obstruction to avoid a crush shot. It is not a crush shot if the other ball in a croquet stroke becomes 'crushed', because it will not have been in contact with the mallet.

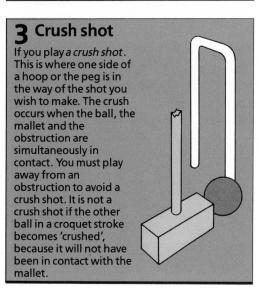

4 Foul croquet

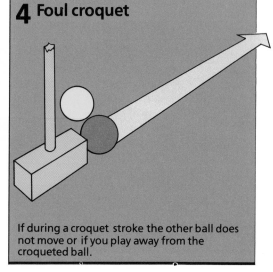

If during a croquet stroke the other ball does not move or if you play away from the croqueted ball.

Wired Balls

A wired ball

If, when it is your turn you find you cannot strike either side extremity of any other ball with your ball either because the hoops or the peg are in the way, or because they obstruct the backswing of your mallet, then your ball is described as 'wired'. In this situation you may lift it and play it from either baulk line provided your ball was played into the position by the opposing team and *not* by yourself or your partner.

You may declare a ball wired even if your partner ball is quite clear.

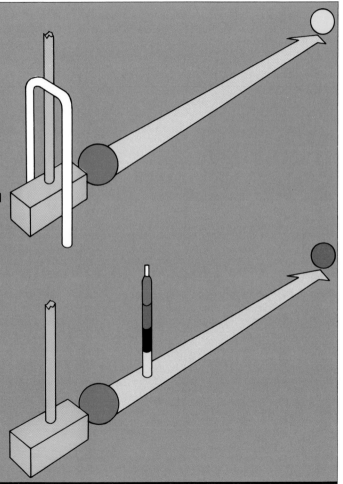

Mallet Stances and Grips

Stance and grip are a matter of choice. Do what feels comfortable. Here are two examples.

The side stance

In this position the left forearm should be almost horizontal. The height of the player will affect the length of mallet handle required. Either the left or the right foot can be forward.

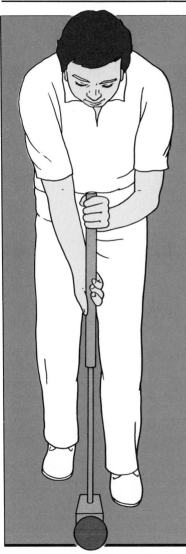

The centre stance

The centre stance requires a little more strength than the side stance. The feet can either be level or one in front of the other. It is generally considered that the centre style gives greater accuracy, but it is very much a matter of personal preference.

Standard grip

The standard grip has the thumb round the top of the shaft and the forefinger of the lower hand running down the back. See the main illustration, left.

The Irish grip

The forefinger of the top hand can be under the little finger of the bottom hand, and so the hands are interlocked.

Basic Croquet Strokes

The drive

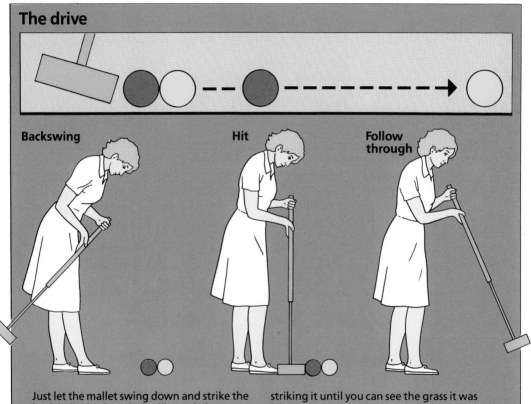

Backswing

Hit

Follow through

Just let the mallet swing down and strike the back ball. The front ball will travel about three or four times further than the back ball.

The relative distances that the two balls travel can be altered by the amount of follow-through of the mallet head.

Always keep your eyes on the ball when striking it until you can see the grass it was lying on.

Before striking any ball make sure you are taking the right line by walking up to it. This is called stalking a ball. Concentrate on the direction you want the ball to go in rather than the line of your mallet.

The roll

If follow-through is increased by pushing at the moment of contact, the back ball will roll much further than in a drive shot. Expert players can make the back ball roll as far as or even further than the front ball. The hands are held lower on the shaft and the player leans forward to drive the balls away. Be careful as you follow through not to fault through double hitting.

The stop shot

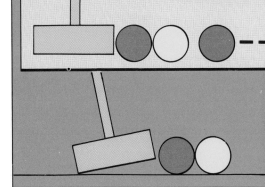

If the mallet head is pulled back at the moment of contact the back ball will move only a short distance. The lighter the mallet the easier this shot is. Some players tilt the mallet face upwards for the shot and ground the mallet at the moment of contact.

Angling the Ball

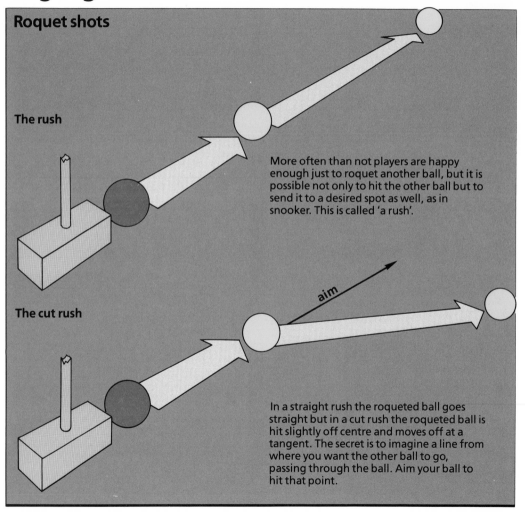

Roquet shots

The rush

More often than not players are happy enough just to roquet another ball, but it is possible not only to hit the other ball but to send it to a desired spot as well, as in snooker. This is called 'a rush'.

The cut rush

aim

In a straight rush the roqueted ball goes straight but in a cut rush the roqueted ball is hit slightly off centre and moves off at a tangent. The secret is to imagine a line from where you want the other ball to go, passing through the ball. Aim your ball to hit that point.

Croquet shots

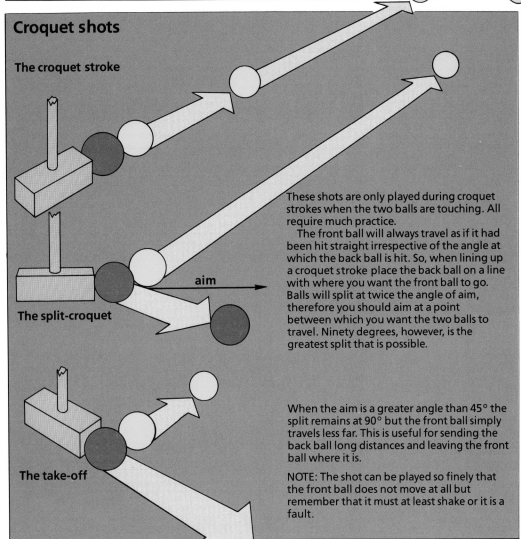

The croquet stroke

The split-croquet

aim

The take-off

These shots are only played during croquet strokes when the two balls are touching. All require much practice.

The front ball will always travel as if it had been hit straight irrespective of the angle at which the back ball is hit. So, when lining up a croquet stroke place the back ball on a line with where you want the front ball to go. Balls will split at twice the angle of aim, therefore you should aim at a point between which you want the two balls to travel. Ninety degrees, however, is the greatest split that is possible.

When the aim is a greater angle than 45° the split remains at 90° but the front ball simply travels less far. This is useful for sending the back ball long distances and leaving the front ball where it is.

NOTE: The shot can be played so finely that the front ball does not move at all but remember that it must at least shake or it is a fault.

Hoop Shots

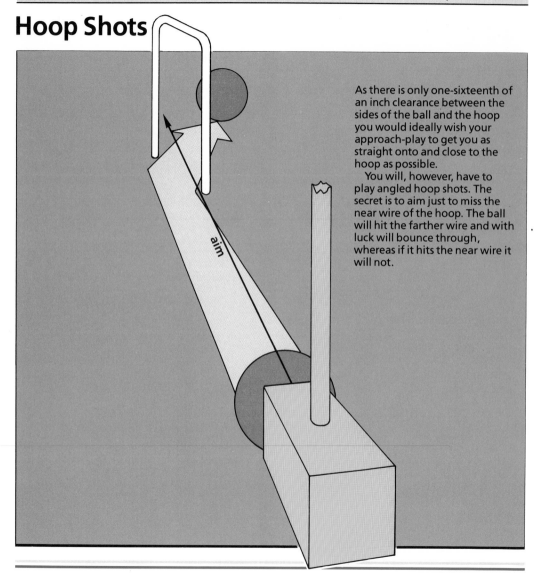

As there is only one-sixteenth of an inch clearance between the sides of the ball and the hoop you would ideally wish your approach-play to get you as straight onto and close to the hoop as possible.

You will, however, have to play angled hoop shots. The secret is to aim just to miss the near wire of the hoop. The ball will hit the farther wire and with luck will bounce through, whereas if it hits the near wire it will not.

Approaching Hoops

An approach to a hoop is most often made with a croquet shot and the hoop is then run using the continuation shot.

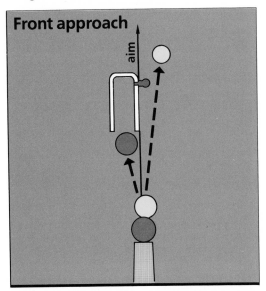

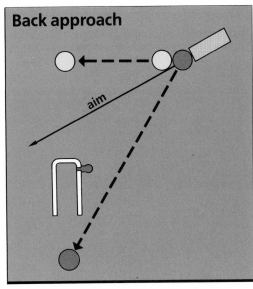

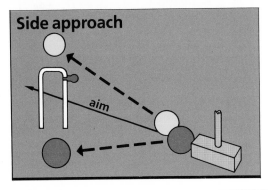

Place the back ball against the front ball so that it forms a line to where you want the front ball to go. Aim the mallet mid-way between where you want the two balls to go. Play a drive, roll or stop shot to achieve the relative distances for the two balls.

Try to leave the croqueted ball in a good position the other side of the hoop so that after running the hoop you have as easy a roquet as possible.

Making a Break

A turn ends after one stroke unless another ball is roqueted or a hoop run, so the more balls that are involved the easier it is to keep a break going.

The two ball break

To describe the basics of a break let us look at how two balls can be manipulated to create scoring chances. It would be possible, although difficult, to extend this break to the next hoop.

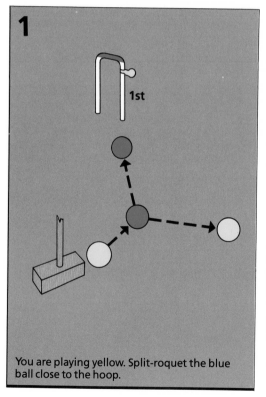

You are playing yellow. Split-roquet the blue ball close to the hoop.

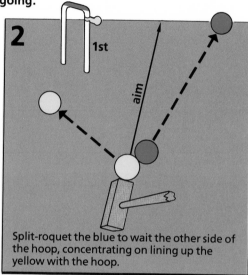

Split-roquet the blue to wait the other side of the hoop, concentrating on lining up the yellow with the hoop.

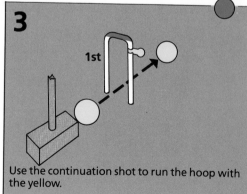

Use the continuation shot to run the hoop with the yellow.

4

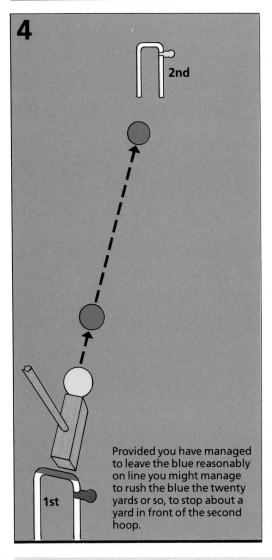

Provided you have managed to leave the blue reasonably on line you might manage to rush the blue the twenty yards or so, to stop about a yard in front of the second hoop.

5

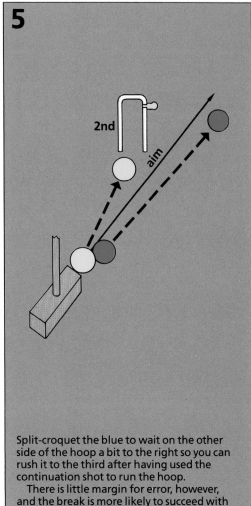

Split-croquet the blue to wait on the other side of the hoop a bit to the right so you can rush it to the third after having used the continuation shot to run the hoop.

There is little margin for error, however, and the break is more likely to succeed with three balls (see over).

The three ball break

Here the first hoop has already been scored using just the yellow and blue but there is the additional advantage of the red ball which can be brought into the break to make life easier. In this case, when the yellow is running the first hoop, the red is called the 'pioneer'.

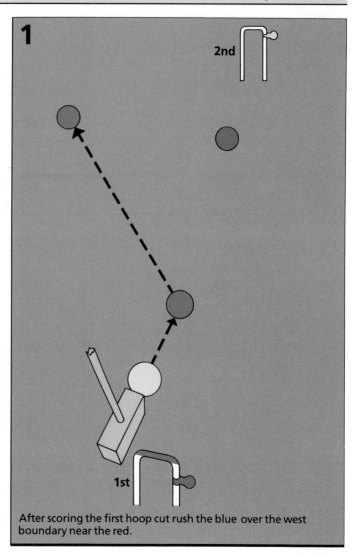

After scoring the first hoop cut rush the blue over the west boundary near the red.

2

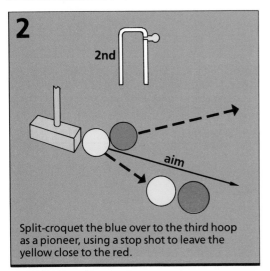

Split-croquet the blue over to the third hoop as a pioneer, using a stop shot to leave the yellow close to the red.

3

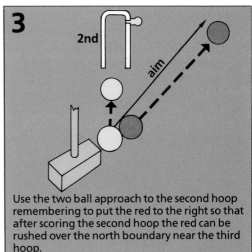

Use the two ball approach to the second hoop remembering to put the red to the right so that after scoring the second hoop the red can be rushed over the north boundary near the third hoop.

4

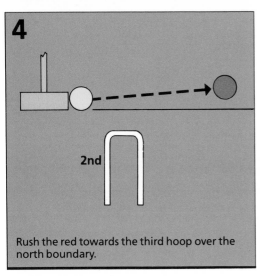

Rush the red towards the third hoop over the north boundary.

5

Croquet the red to the fourth to act as pioneer leaving the yellow close to the blue, and approach and score the third hoop in the usual manner. With any luck by sending a pioneer ball to the next hoop but one each time, you might get round but it is even easier with four balls.

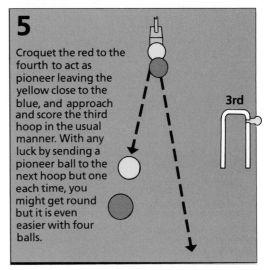

The four ball break

This is by far the easiest of breaks and once a certain level of skill has been acquired can result in the running of several hoops.

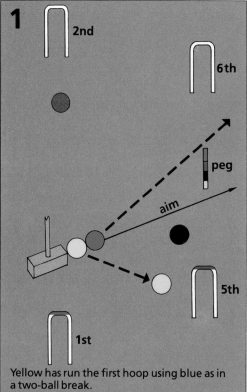

Yellow has run the first hoop using blue as in a two-ball break.

Now instead of having to run blue off the west boundary as in a three-ball break, blue is instead gently roqueted. With the croquet stroke blue is sent to the third hoop as a pioneer and yellow uses the continuation shot for a simple roquet on black.

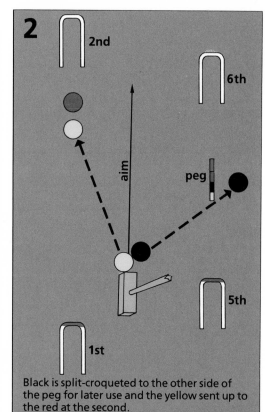

Black is split-croqueted to the other side of the peg for later use and the yellow sent up to the red at the second.

The red is gently roqueted using the continuation shot.

3

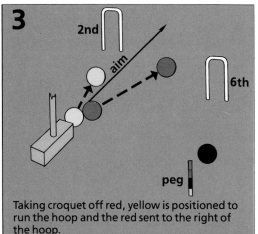

Taking croquet off red, yellow is positioned to run the hoop and the red sent to the right of the hoop.

The hoop is run on the continuation shot.

4

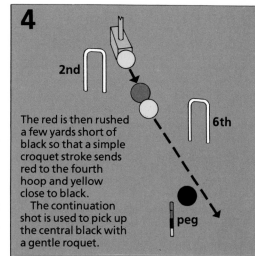

The red is then rushed a few yards short of black so that a simple croquet stroke sends red to the fourth hoop and yellow close to black.

The continuation shot is used to pick up the central black with a gentle roquet.

5

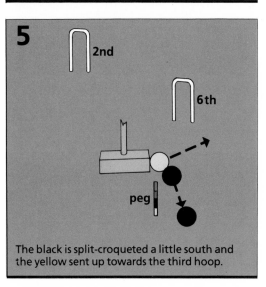

The black is split-croqueted a little south and the yellow sent up towards the third hoop.

6

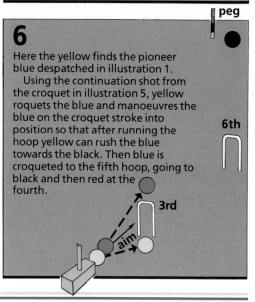

Here the yellow finds the pioneer blue despatched in illustration 1.

Using the continuation shot from the croquet in illustration 5, yellow roquets the blue and manoeuvres the blue on the croquet stroke into position so that after running the hoop yellow can rush the blue towards the black. Then blue is croqueted to the fifth hoop, going to black and then red at the fourth.

Opening Sequences

The first two turns of each team are used to play the balls onto the court from anywhere on either of the two baulk lines.

To get the game off to a quick start, beginners should go for the first hoop. More experienced players should, however, resist this temptation. The hoop is eighteen feet away and the clearance on either side of the ball is only one-sixteenth of an inch. Success is

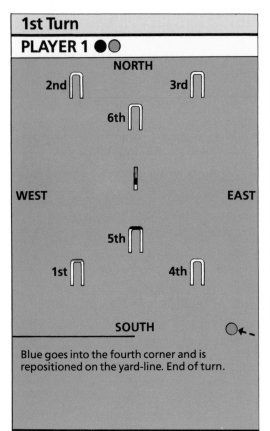

1st Turn

PLAYER 1 ●○

Blue goes into the fourth corner and is repositioned on the yard-line. End of turn.

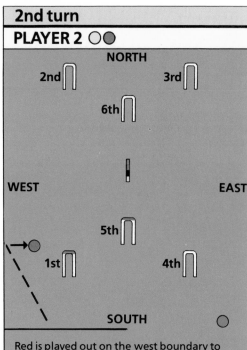

2nd turn

PLAYER 2 ○○

Red is played out on the west boundary to avoid giving black an easy roquet. End of turn. This ball is only ten yards away and can entice Player 1 to attempt to roquet it with the next shot. For this reason it is known as 'a Tice'.

therefore unlikely. Much more likely is that the ball will stick halfway through or bounce back off the hoop.

Your opponent, whose turn it will now be, has much more chance of hitting your ball than you did of running the hoop. Worse still, having roqueted your ball and approached the hoop with a split croquet shot, the chances of your opponent scoring will be excellent. For this reason most players open by playing off to the sides.

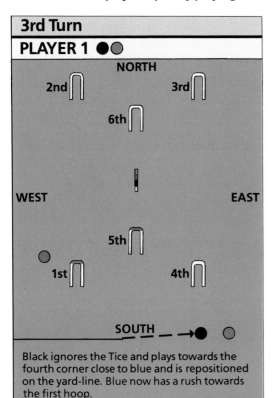

3rd Turn
PLAYER 1 ●○

Black ignores the Tice and plays towards the fourth corner close to blue and is repositioned on the yard-line. Blue now has a rush towards the first hoop.

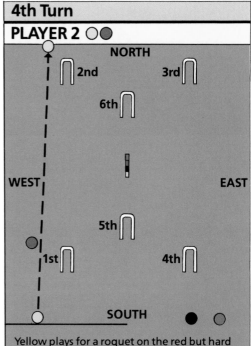

4th Turn
PLAYER 2 ○●

Yellow plays for a roquet on the red but hard enough so that if it misses it goes safely to the second corner. If yellow hits the red, however, it is possible to build a break on the fourth turn. See next page.

A Break on the Fourth Turn

It is possible for a fairly good player to make a break on the fourth turn.

Let us assume that yellow hits red. It will be travelling fast so red will probably go out of play. How will yellow build up a break?

First/Second/Third shot

PLAYER 4 ●○

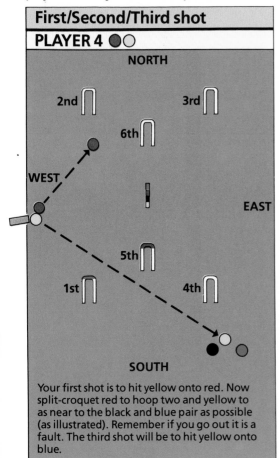

Your first shot is to hit yellow onto red. Now split-croquet red to hoop two and yellow to as near to the black and blue pair as possible (as illustrated). Remember if you go out it is a fault. The third shot will be to hit yellow onto blue.

Fourth shot

PLAYER 4 ●○

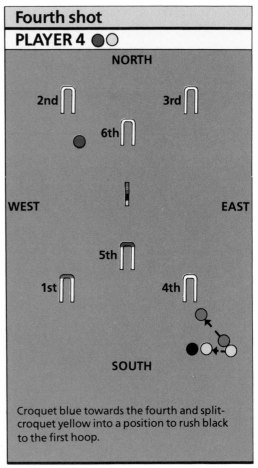

Croquet blue towards the fourth and split-croquet yellow into a position to rush black to the first hoop.

Fifth shot

PLAYER 4 ●○

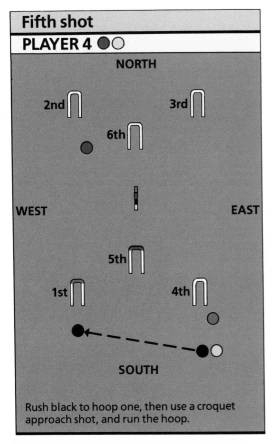

Rush black to hoop one, then use a croquet approach shot, and run the hoop.

Playing safe

PLAYER 4 ●○

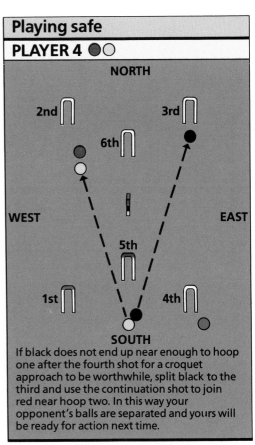

If black does not end up near enough to hoop one after the fourth shot for a croquet approach to be worthwhile, split black to the third and use the continuation shot to join red near hoop two. In this way your opponent's balls are separated and yours will be ready for action next time.

If the fifth shot succeeds and the first hoop is run successfully, then the red can be brought into play for a three-ball break. See page 30.

A Break on the Fifth Turn

This is a very difficult series of shots which would only normally be played by an advanced player but it is useful to illustrate how an expert might approach the situation. Red and yellow are as in the break on the fourth turn, as is blue, but black is further across near the east boundary.

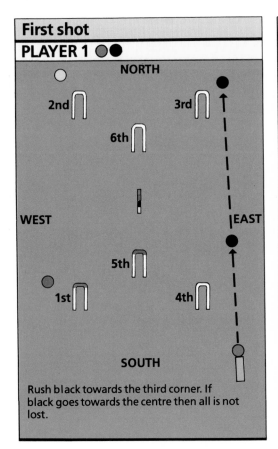

First shot

Rush black towards the third corner. If black goes towards the centre then all is not lost.

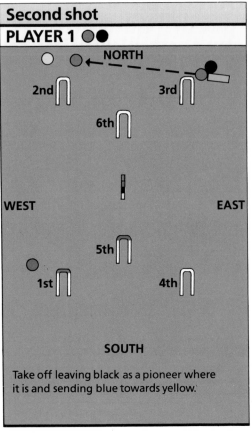

Second shot

Take off leaving black as a pioneer where it is and sending blue towards yellow.

Third shot
PLAYER 1 ○●

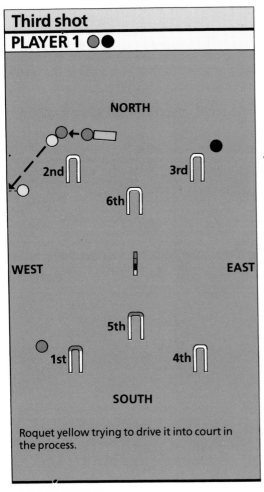

Roquet yellow trying to drive it into court in the process.

Fourth Shot
PLAYER 1 ○●

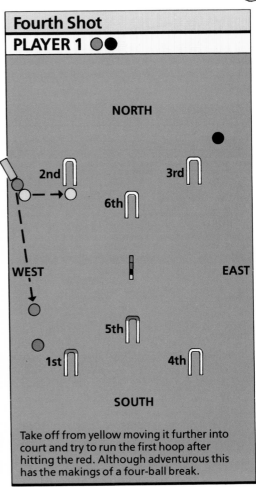

Take off from yellow moving it further into court and try to run the first hoop after hitting the red. Although adventurous this has the makings of a four-ball break.

Playing safe

If the approach to hoop one with red does not go well, return blue to black in the third corner leaving yellow and red widely separated.

Laying -Up

Laying-up is playing safe. If you find your break is not working out or you encounter a difficulty you had not anticipated, instead of missing a risky shot (leaving your balls in an ideal position for your opponent to poach a break) use your last shot to rearrange things to your advantage.

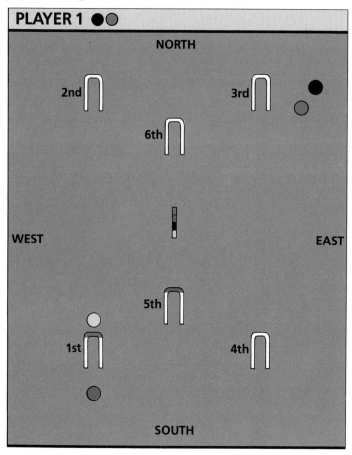

PLAYER 1 ●○

NORTH

2nd

3rd

6th

WEST   EAST

5th

1st

4th

SOUTH

Wired for rushing

You have left your blue and black balls in a perfect position for a rush. You have also left your opponent's balls wired from each other at your next hoop (although obviously not if it is also your opponent's next hoop).

Make sure, however, you do not leave either of your opponent's balls completely wired (i.e. they are unable to see either black or blue) as they can pick up and play from either baulk. See page 19.

PLAYER 1 ●○

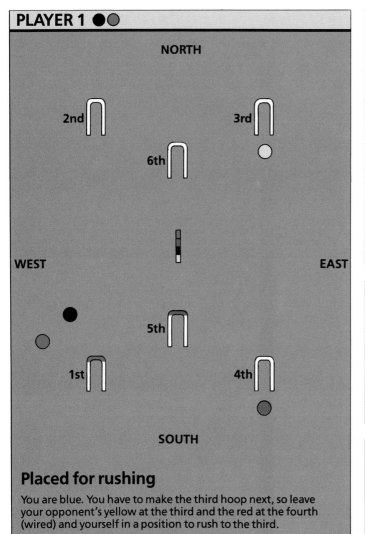

NORTH

2nd

3rd

6th

WEST

EAST

5th

1st

4th

SOUTH

Placed for rushing

You are blue. You have to make the third hoop next, so leave your opponent's yellow at the third and the red at the fourth (wired) and yourself in a position to rush to the third.

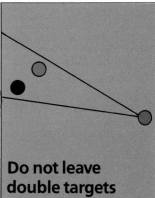

Do not leave double targets

When laying up a rush for yourself make sure you do not leave a two-ball target for your opponent.

Set up a backward ball

If one of your balls has run more hoops than the other it is called 'forward' and the other, 'backward'. Generally lay-up for your backward ball.

Force a forward play

Lay-up in such a way that your opponent is obliged to play the turn with the forward ball instead of the backward one.

Pegging-Out

Only balls which have gone through the rover hoop (the twelfth in a long game, the sixth in a short game) can peg-out. This is achieved by the ball touching the peg. Once pegged-out a ball is removed from the court. For this reason it is not a good idea to peg-out one ball until the other is also a rover otherwise you play the rest of the game with one ball to your opponent's two.

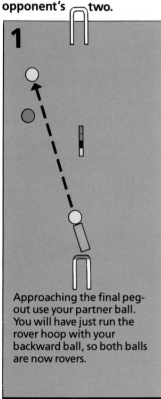

1

Approaching the final peg-out use your partner ball. You will have just run the rover hoop with your backward ball, so both balls are now rovers.

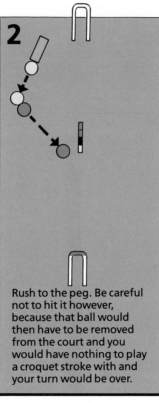

2

Rush to the peg. Be careful not to hit it however, because that ball would then have to be removed from the court and you would have nothing to play a croquet stroke with and your turn would be over.

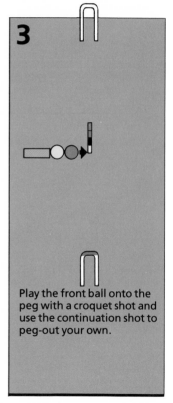

3

Play the front ball onto the peg with a croquet shot and use the continuation shot to peg-out your own.

If both you and your opponent have rover balls either may peg-out the other. Sometimes if you are well advanced with both balls and your opponent has a very backward ball it can be an advantage to peg-out the opponent's ball. Only if your ball is a rover may you peg-out an opponent's rover.

Coming in from the cold

The croquet court is large and if you have been standing as the out-player for some time it can be difficult to see what it is best to do when it is your turn. Here are some guidelines:-

1 If you find yourself victim of a lay-up you should always play with the ball that has been left at your opponent's next hoop.

5 If your opponent has left a ball near one of your hoops play the ball for that hoop even if it is well forward.

2 If both are at your opponent's hoops play the ball which is at his backward ball's hoop.

6 When shooting at an opponent's ball remember if it is on the yard-line and you miss you will end up on the yard-line next to it.

3 If your opponent has left a ball near to one of yours play that ball.

7 If your opponent has layed up a rush you have little to lose by aiming for it.

4 If there is no real advantage anywhere else always play your backward ball.

8 Try and get to your other ball if your opponent's balls are well separated. If there is nothing positive to be played for play to the maximum disadvantage of your opponent.

Handicaps

Handicapping players enables good players to play with beginners on a more equal footing. Poor players are awarded 'bisques', which are in effect free turns. Players can have as many as 24 in club play, but the maximum in tournaments is 18.

If you break down when building a break, instead of losing your turn use one of your bisques. You must play the same ball with the bisque as you did on the turn.

There is an interesting rule governing bisques. If you say you are intending to use one you may change your mind, but if you say you are not you cannot revoke your decision.

Bad Habits

After a few months of playing croquet it is easy to develop some or all of the following bad habits. Being aware of what they are will make it easier to correct them as early as possible.

1 Lifting the head

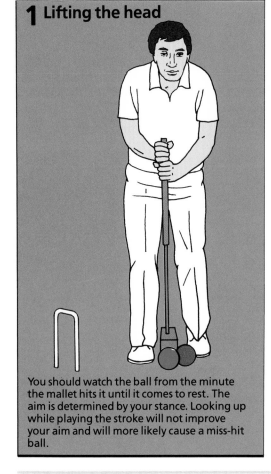

You should watch the ball from the minute the mallet hits it until it comes to rest. The aim is determined by your stance. Looking up while playing the stroke will not improve your aim and will more likely cause a miss-hit ball.

2 Crooked backswing

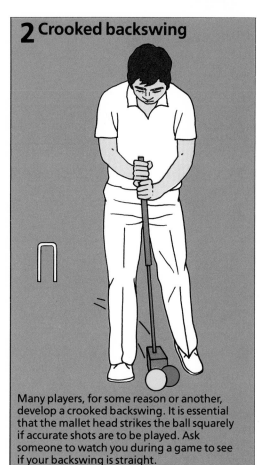

Many players, for some reason or another, develop a crooked backswing. It is essential that the mallet head strikes the ball squarely if accurate shots are to be played. Ask someone to watch you during a game to see if your backswing is straight.

3 Not stalking the ball

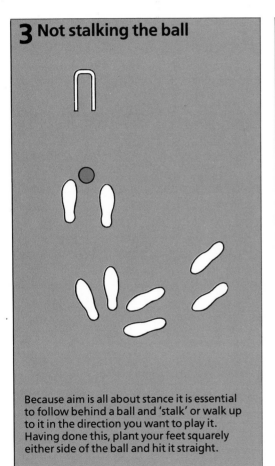

Because aim is all about stance it is essential to follow behind a ball and 'stalk' or walk up to it in the direction you want to play it. Having done this, plant your feet squarely either side of the ball and hit it straight.

4 Hogging play in doubles

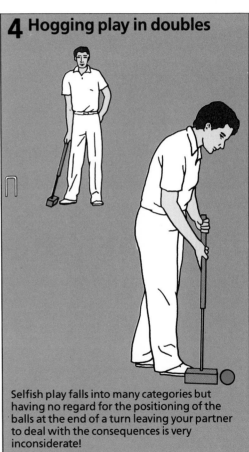

Selfish play falls into many categories but having no regard for the positioning of the balls at the end of a turn leaving your partner to deal with the consequences is very inconsiderate!

Practising

Croquet is an ideal game for practising alone. Here are some simple practices which will improve your game.

1 Pairs

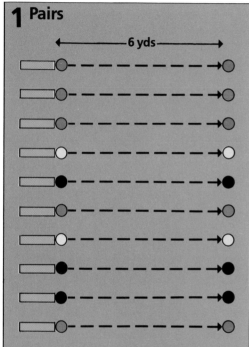

Line up ten balls six yards or so from another ten balls. Take the first ball and see if you can hit the ball lined up opposite it. Then move on to the second pair and so on. Make a mental note of how many pairs you managed before missing. When you practise next time, set up the pairs again and again until you beat your previous score.

2 Rushing to the peg

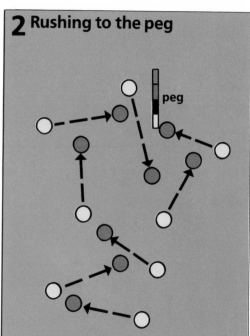

Start at the south baulk with two balls – one on the line, one three feet inside the court. Playing only rushes, rush the ball in court to the peg. This is excellent practice. If you miss a shot, start again.

3 Round the clock

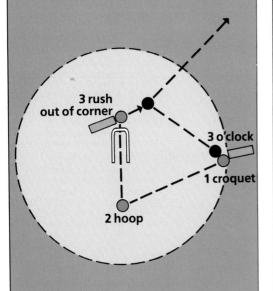

Start anywhere within six feet of one of the corner hoops. Play a croquet approach shot, run the hoop, then rush the other ball out of the corner between the yard markers. Start at twelve o'clock and repeat at one o'clock, 2 o'clock etc until you have gone 'round the clock'. The illustration shows the sequence starting at 3 o'clock.

4 Three- and four-ball breaks

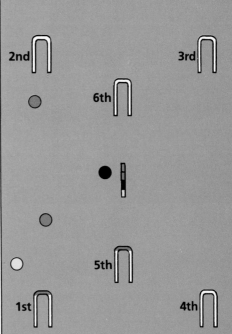

Beginners often find they create breaks only to fail to capitalize on them. Set up a three- or four-ball break and practise (if necessary replaying a shot several times) making as many hoops as possible. You can also try positioning the balls randomly and try to work out how you might construct a break. This is excellent for learning the basic logic of croquet.

Glossary

BAULK — North or south; the two lines one yard in from the north and south boundaries from which the game can begin or to which 'wired' balls may be removed and played.

BISQUE — Free turn awarded to poorer players in handicap games. Bisques may be used any time a turn breaks down. The maximum number of bisques is twenty-four in club play, eighteen in tournaments.

CROQUET STROKE — The shot which must be played after any roquet. The player's ball is picked up and placed touching the roqueted ball. The player's ball is then struck with the mallet. The other ball must appreciably move or it is a foul stroke.

CRUSH SHOT — A foul shot in which the mallet, the player's ball and a hoop are all in contact simultaneously.

CUT RUSH — A roquet shot in which the roqueted ball is deliberately hit off-centre so that it goes off at an angle to a desired position.

DRIVE — A croquet shot in which a player's ball and the roqueted ball travel their natural distances. The roqueted ball will travel approximately three to four times further.

LAY-UP — To use the last shot or two of a turn to leave the balls in positions as disadvantageous to your opponent as possible, but favourable to yourself.

PEG — The central wooden peg which is the ultimate target for all balls. When a ball hits the peg it is 'pegged out' and removed from the court.

ROLL — A croquet shot in which the player's ball travels nearly as far as the roqueted ball. This is achieved by pushing through at the moment of contact.

ROQUET — When the player's ball strikes any of the other balls. A croquet stroke must then be played.

ROVER — The last hoop before the peg. Once a ball has run the last hoop it is known as a 'rover' and can peg itself out or peg out other rover balls.

RUSH — A roquet shot in which the roqueted ball is deliberately knocked to a desired position.

SPLIT-CROQUET — A croquet shot in which the player's ball is hit at an angle to the roqueted ball so that their paths diverge. The angle of divergence is twice that of the angle of aim. Once the aim exceeds 45°, however, the divergence remains at 90° and the croqueted ball travels less far.

STOP SHOT — A croquet shot in which the player's ball hardly moves at all due to no follow-through with the mallet.

TAKE-OFF — A croquet shot in which the player's ball is struck at right angles to the croqueted ball so that the croqueted ball barely moves.

TURN — The duration for which a player can legally play a ball.

WIRED BALL — A ball which is so positioned by the opponent that if hit in a straight line it cannot hit any other ball without striking a hoop or the peg. Wired balls can be picked up and played from either baulk.